HELP!

I'M LIVING WITH TERMINAL ILLNESS

Reggie Weems

Consulting Editor: Dr. Paul Tautges

© Day One Publications 2012

First printed 2012

ISBN 978-1-84625-319-5

All Bible quotations, unless stated otherwise, are from The Holy Bible, English Standard Version. Copyright © 2001 by Crossway Bibles, a division of Good News Publishers.

Published by Day One Publications
Ryelands Road, Leominster, HR6 8NZ

TEL 01568 613 740 FAX 01568 611 473

email—sales@dayone.co.uk

UK web site—www.dayone.co.uk

USA web site—www.dayonebookstore.com

Designed by **documen**
Printed by Orchard Press Cheltenham Ltd

Contents

INTRODUCTION

I began writing this booklet the same week Jenny[1] returned home to Northeast Tennessee from Florida after her release from a medical trial. Participation in the trial was dependent on her cancer responding to treatment, so her discharge from the program said everything that words could not verbalize and that many hearts did not want to believe. Less than a week after my wife and I, with several friends, welcomed her home at the airport, Jenny died.

Jenny had been diagnosed with pancreatic cancer five years earlier and had endured chemotherapy, surgery, and several clinical trials in efforts to minimize the effects of living with what was, in her case, an inoperable disease. But the reactions of her and her husband, Stan, to God's ways and timing assured everyone who witnessed their suffering that divine grace is sufficient.

1 Names have been changed to protect the identities of those concerned.

They both knew the truth of these words:

> *My Father's way may twist and turn,*
> *My heart may throb and ache,*
> *But in my soul I'm glad to know,*
> *He maketh no mistake.*
>
> *My cherished plans may go astray,*
> *My hopes may fade away,*
> *But I'll trust my Lord to lead*
> *For He doth know the way.*
>
> *Tho' night be dark, and it may seem*
> *That day will never break,*
> *I'll pin my faith, my all in Him,*
> *He maketh no mistake.*
>
> *There's so much now I cannot see,*
> *My eyesight's far too dim;*
> *But come what may, I'll simply trust*
> *And leave it all to Him.*
>
> *For by and by the mist will lift*
> *And plain it all He'll make,*
> *Through all the way, tho' dark to me*
> *He made not one mistake.*[2]

There are many ways the subject of terminal illness

could be approached. The title of this booklet says a lot about my personal perspective on living and dying and how I plan to engage with the issue of terminal illness. It is not *Help! I'm Dying from Terminal Illness* but *Help! I'm Living with Terminal Illness*. This perspective is, I believe, beneficial to anyone suffering with—or concerned about someone suffering with— terminal illness. My hope is to encourage any dying person, or such a person's family member or friend, with a singular hope which the dying process cannot diminish and death cannot extinguish.

Eighteenth-century preacher John Wesley once said, "Our people die well because they live well."[3] Jenny lived and died with grace, dignity, faith, and joy. Given the time and opportunity, Stan and Jenny could easily have written this booklet. It is to Stan and to Jenny's memory that this booklet is lovingly dedicated.

2 A. M. Overton, "He Maketh No Mistake," quoted in Lee Roberson, *The Gold Mine* (Murfreesboro, TN: The Sword of the Lord, 1996), 109–110.
3 Quoted in Leon O. Hynson, *Through Faith to Understanding: Wesleyan Essays on Vital Christianity* (Lexington, KY: Emeth Press, 2005), 141.

Life and Death Are Personal

Death is very personal to us all. I well remember receiving the news of my grandfather's impending death. His prognosis was twelve months and he died within weeks of that prediction. Only a few days before his death my family traveled to see him. Although bedbound, he held my first child and laughed with her when she was a mere six months old. But it grieved my heart that my grandfather never enjoyed my children as he had the children of my older cousins.

A similar grief has probably motivated you to read about terminal illness. Grief is a real, God-given, necessary emotion and should not be denied. Grief has its purposes, but in the battle of emotions it should not win the day. This booklet is really about grieving with joy and hope.

My parents had anticipated a life of leisurely travel

in their retirement years, but my father's illness permanently canceled those plans. He suffered from a decade-long fight with Chronic Obstructive Pulmonary Disease (COPD), a debilitating respiratory illness which inhibits breathing. As the disease progresses, less air flows in and out of the airways. For many years he was unable to walk the length of a room without intermittent stops. His inability to breathe often required him to live dependent on an external supply of oxygen. Visits to the local hospital emergency room became so habitual and lengthy that my mother routinely dropped him off at the ER, returned home, and awaited the call to retrieve him.

Dad never complained about his illness, but he worried about how and when he would die. A defibrillating pacemaker often reminded his heart to beat, but not without great physical pain. I vividly remember my sister's phone call encouraging our family to make our way to San Antonio as my dad entered an ICU for the last time. The inevitable had become unavoidable—as it does for us all, sooner or later.

Many things can be said about death. It is universal and is perhaps the most conspicuous thing that is wrong with this world. The mortality rate is 100 percent. For this reason, no one profits from denying the inevitability of death. Yet any discussion about it is difficult. My most important counsel to you is to find your strength, joy, and hope in God and in his Word, the Bible. God's Word is true, sufficient, and relevant to everything about us. God does not avoid the difficult issues of life. The Bible explains life, suffering, and death, and in particular speaks clearly and directly to end-of-life concerns. This is one of the reasons I most appreciate the Christian gospel. It is a very powerful anchor of truth and rationality for anyone in any kind of storm. We'll turn our attention to these important matters in the next chapter.

There are, however, other, practical matters to consider in this process. While it is not my intent to address medical concerns regarding end-of-life care, I would encourage you to consult with your pastor, family, friends, and physician and to do so in timeliness and candor. If you are a Christian you can speak directly and honestly about death, because you know that for the Christian, death is God's release from the curse of sin. In addition, please do not ignore the advice of those who are further along this path or the wisdom of professionals who have walked through this valley with others.

The following action points were derived from

conversations with health-care and mental-health professionals as well as friends enduring the dying process.

Planning Care

▶ Death is an extremely emotive issue. The people around you may not know how to begin talking with you about it. Take the initiative to openly and candidly speak about end-of-life concerns. It is also important to gain your family's agreement on essential issues. Conduct private conversations if disagreement exists. You will not want to spend this important time in estrangement from those closest to you. Take the necessary time to encourage everyone to respect your decisions.

▶ Do your best to be open and clear about your wishes regarding medical care, financial concerns, your will, your funeral, and life after your death. Explain what caused you to make certain decisions. How do your decisions give meaning to your life and death?

▶ Share your end-of-life concerns. Do you desire independence? What will happen if or when you cannot remain independent? If this happens, with whom or how will you live? Would you prefer to die at home?

▶ Is there a hospice care facility in your vicinity?[4] If so, I would encourage you to use their services. As a former board member of a local hospice and the husband of a former hospice nurse I know that hospice personnel combine professionalism and compassion in a unique way as they care for patients and families.

▶ If you currently have no ongoing Christian influence in your life, I recommend that you contact an evangelical minister of the gospel. He will certainly be willing to visit with you and your family to offer biblical counsel. Ask someone you love to call a Bible-believing, Bible-teaching church in your area to inquire for a pastoral visit.

▶ Do you have a living will or advanced directives that detail your medical preferences? Both will speak to the specifics of your medical care if you are unable to speak for yourself.

4 For a very helpful discussion of the benefits of hospice, see Deborah Howard, *Help! Someone I Love Has Cancer*, also available from Day One.

▶ Consider creating a durable power of attorney. It allows someone else to act on your behalf when you are unable to do so. A durable power of attorney can go into effect as soon as you sign it, when you deem it appropriate, or when a doctor confirms you are incapacitated. As long as you are mentally competent, you can revoke a durable power of attorney anytime you wish.

▶ Of course, every decision is subject to change. Maintain open lines of communication and keep the conversation going with your family and other significant people in your life. Your openness and frankness will encourage the same from others. Many important and meaningful discussions can be held during this time. You and everyone around you will benefit from the transparency you exhibit.

Funeral and Business Arrangements

▶ Have you written a final will? A will enables you to retain control about what remains of your life even after your death. It protects those you love. A will can also ensure that your last wishes are fulfilled.

13

▶ What about funeral arrangements? Nothing adequately prepares us for the death of someone we love. Feelings of panic can paralyze those who remain. A prearranged funeral can serve many purposes. If you are a Christian it can share your faith, and it provides closure for loved ones, relieves your loved ones of the responsibility of its planning, honors your last requests, and enables those you love to exert their energy and emotion on the care of one another.

▶ Consider writing your own obituary. You know best what is important to be said about you. Your obituary is a history of your life and a lasting legacy of your values, priorities, triumphs, and joys.

▶ Take time to locate and share important documents. Your family may need your birth and marriage certificates, divorce decrees, car and property titles, life insurance or health insurance policies, summary of pensions or benefits, and death certificates of any loved ones who have preceded you in death.

▶ It is important that you and your family understand in advance what your insurance will cover for your care. Have you researched this?

▶ Make a financial inventory of all your assets and debts. Write down all important information such as bank account numbers and passwords, e-mail addresses and passwords, the deed of trust to your home, the location of safety deposit boxes, and the name of your attorney. Gather your bills and give someone the oversight of paying your monthly expenses, such as your utilities.

▶ If applicable, it is imperative that someone notify the Social Security department, Medicare or other governmental agencies of your death. Who will assume this responsibility?

Emotional and Relational Needs

▶ You may notice that life tires you more easily each day. To recuperate and ensure you enjoy time with family and friends, consider time limits for visits from those outside your immediate family, take naps throughout the day, and discover new activities that do not require as much energy.

▶ You are also going to experience emotional changes, such as denial, anger, fear, and grief,

15

if you are not already doing so. Don't hesitate to discuss your feelings with your pastor or family. In reality, your family members want to talk to you about their grief and fears. Talk with someone else who has a terminal illness for mutual encouragement.

▶ Consider writing down all the difficult experiences of your life in the past and how you coped with them. Doing so may encourage you about your illness. You may also remember something of value that will help you now.

▶ Is there anyone in particular whom you want to contact soon? Consider calling old friends to rejoice in your relationship or to say goodbye. Death has a way of helping us get over former grievances. Perhaps you could heal a broken relationship or become reconciled to those with whom you have had disagreements.

▶ Make a list of people you want to be contacted when you die. This list could include the phone numbers or e-mail addresses of extended family, friends, social acquaintances, or former coworkers.

I trust that these suggestions will give you mental, emotional, and physical rest as you handle the dying process, and will enable you and your family to concentrate on loving one another rather than being distracted by peripheral issues.

Understanding Why We Die

Opinions about life and death are as numerous as the people who espouse them. For Mary Baker Eddy, the founder of the Christian Science religion, reality existed beyond the material senses in what she coined "the infinite mind." From her perspective, fear and its mental repercussions were the only cause of any physical malady. Eddy sincerely thought that if "the infinite mind" could be accessed, all fears—intellectual and emotional—could be removed. Faith, conviction, and expectation could then replace fear, resulting in the certain healing of any disease or sickness. Ultimately, even death could be denied its victory over life. Sadly, Eddy died December 3, 1910, her teaching proven false, her faith in "the infinite mind" a failure, and her hopes unrealized.

Contrary to Mary Baker Eddy's attempt to dismiss sickness and death, the Bible doesn't pull any punches about their reality, cause, consequences, or cure. From the Christian perspective, God *is*—and that changes everything. Such a divine backdrop for all existence provides an immovable hope in the midst of any circumstance. In addition, everything humans need to know about life, death, and beyond is addressed with clarity in the sixty-six books of the Holy Bible, the unique revelation from God. Like Mary Baker Eddy, many people attempt to address humanity's fallen situation with differing, even opposing, viewpoints. But only the Bible assesses the human condition with an accuracy that matches the reality with which we live. The Bible defines what it means to be human and to live and die.

The Bible is truthful and accurate on all the matters it addresses. For this reason it does not encourage people to pretend that death is not real. Nor does it diminish the effect death has on human beings. In fact, Scripture encourages us to do everything possible to be aware of and prepare for death. Someone has even used "Bible" as an acronym of "Basic Instructions Before Leaving Earth." Thus in the Bible God warns,

> It is appointed for man to die once, and
> after that comes judgment.
>
> (Hebrews 9:27)

Death Is the Consequence of Sin

The Bible states that sin is the real cause of death. Death is natural only in a fallen world. It was not natural to the Garden of Eden, created by God at the beginning of time. The repercussions of the first sin committed there are still felt in the various secondary causes of our deaths through heart attack, cancer, stroke, COPD, pneumonia, renal failure, and so on. Sin may seem to be an odd topic for an end-of-life discussion. In reality, it is an important matter at any stage of life, but especially as one nears the end of life.

Spirituality can construct a platform for hope, but as Mary Baker Eddy's "faith" evidenced, that hope is not always valid. Real and sufficient faith is only in the person and finished work of Jesus Christ. Any other faith will betray you. And before the Christian gospel becomes good news, it is necessarily preceded by the bad news of our sin. This makes the good news of salvation in Jesus *really* good news.

Death entered human history as God's forewarned

judgment on sin. Adam and Eve knew that their disobedience would result in their demise. Romans 5:12 explains that

> Sin came into the world through one man,
> and death through sin, and so death spread
> to all men because all sinned.

Since Eden, "the wages of sin [has been] death" (Romans 6:23a), and all men and women "have sinned and fall short of the glory of God" (Romans 3:23). Biblically speaking, the universality of death proves the universality of sin.

During his final illness, King Louis XV of France would apparently not allow his closest advisors to use the word "death" in his presence. But rebuffing its reality did not prevent his death. It did not do so for King Louis XV and it does not do so for anyone else.

Everyone dies because everyone is born a sinner. It might be argued that some people are "innocent" of sin, but in that scenario we're really debating degrees of sin. We can always find someone who is more morally bankrupt than we imagine ourselves to be. Yet any honest person will confess to wrongdoing, that misconduct for which the human

21

language possesses a constellation of words. The Bible simply calls it *sin*. Sin is any offense of self-indulgence against the God who created us for his purposes. That transgression opened the door to death for humans and the rest of creation.[5]

In the opening scenes of the Bible, God reveals himself as the Creator of all things (Genesis 1–2). Creation in general, and human life in particular, says a lot about God. Life itself is a gift from a loving, beneficent Creator. Humans were made by God, exist for God, are responsible to God, and will return back to God. The Bible also quickly reveals God to be holy and righteous. At the very beginning God disclosed himself to be a holy Creator who has the sovereign right to set the standards for human living. At some point in their lives in Eden, Adam and Eve knowingly and willingly violated God's law, a law that was intended for their best interests. Nonetheless, our first parents sided with a voice other than God's and suffered the repercussions of denying God's wisdom as Creator. The deaths of our first parents proved God's sovereign authority over creation.

---

5 People are often concerned about the eternal well-being of infants and children who die. This concern prompted me to write *Help! My Baby Has Died*, also available from Day One.

God Provided the Cure through Jesus Christ

The Bible does not minimize the effects of sin or the reality of death. Neither does it discuss the subject without providing hope in God. The first part of Romans 6:23, which states that "the wages of sin is death," is met with its divine counterpart in the latter portion of that very same verse:

> ... but the free gift of God is eternal life in
> Christ Jesus our Lord.

God did not leave Adam and Eve—or their posterity—to sin's eternally damning consequences. He pursued them, in spite of their attempts to hide from him. God's response to our sin is love poured out on a cross in the person of his Son reconciling the world to himself. In Jesus he accomplished what no human being could ever do: God satisfied the demands of his own justice and demonstrated his genuine love for sinners like you and me.

> *O long and dark the stairs I trod*
> *With trembling feet to find my God.*
> *Gaining a foothold, bit by bit,*

Then slipping back and losing it.
Never progressing, striving still
With weakening grasp and faltering will,
Bleeding to climb to God, while
He serenely smiled, not noting me.
Then came a certain time when
I loosened my hold and fell thereby;
Down to the lowest step my fall,
As if I had not climbed at all.
Now when I lay despairing there,
Listen ... a footfall on the stair.
On that same stair where I afraid,
Faltered and fell and lay dismayed.
And lo, when hope had ceased to be,
My God came down the stairs to me.[6]

God's love for humanity is a most astonishing reality. It changes everything about our existence now and forever. The cross of Jesus transforms death from a horrible end into a glorious beginning.

It was on that cross that God, who is wholly righteous, took the place of those who had wronged him. In Jesus, he suffered the consequences of our

6 Anonymous; cited in John MacArthur, *Romans 1–8* (MacArthur New Testament Commentary; Chicago: Moody, 1991), p. xiii.

transgression. Although it was our sin that took the life of his Son, Jesus willingly sacrificed himself to provide eternal life for all who repent and believe on him. The apostle Paul put it like this:

> For our sake he made him to be sin who
> knew no sin, so that in him we might
> become the righteousness of God.
> (2 Corinthians 5:21)

God's love cost him the life of his Son so that eternal life could be entirely free for all who will come to him to receive it. No one can attain everlasting life. It can only be obtained "by grace ... through faith" (Ephesians 2:8). Scripture emphatically states that God saves us,

> not because of works done by us in
> righteousness, but according to his
> own mercy.
> (Titus 3:5)

The good news is that in Christ God satisfied his demands for perfection. More than that, he credits the perfection of Jesus to those who repent and believe in Jesus Christ. As a result, God now sees believers "in Christ," that is, possessing Christ's perfection. He also treats us accordingly. Sinners who trust in Jesus are therefore free from condemnation. The apostle Paul writes,

> There is therefore now no condemnation for those who are in Christ Jesus.
>
> (Romans 8:1)

Through the cross God remained righteous. Sin was appropriately judged. The cross enables God to offer mercy because our sins are forgiven through Jesus's sacrificial death. Because our sin was against an infinite God, the repercussions were infinite. Only an infinite person could satisfy the infinite cost involved in making us right with God. As such, no human being could have done what Jesus did. Only God could satisfy God, and he did so in Christ.

We are declared righteous in God's sight all—and only—because of what Jesus accomplished on the cross. He exchanged his righteousness for our unrighteousness, his life for our lives. God himself delivered us from his own wrath so that we could be eternally saved rather than eternally condemned. Our sin has been covered by his blood and also taken away by that same act.

Because Jesus had no sin of his own he did not remain in the grave. His resurrection to the Father's right hand publicly displayed the certainty of God's favor and our eternal well-being (Romans 4:25). Christians live because Christ died and rose again. Christians will live forever in heaven because Christ lives forever in an omnipotent reign over sin and death.

It Is All of Grace

Certainly there is no human explanation for what God has done. No one deserves such grace. But God chose a Hebrew word, *hesed*, to describe throughout the Scriptures his unmerited, indefinable kindness.[7] Multiple words in English are employed in an attempt to translate this word that expresses God's relentless pursuit of sinners: love, loyal love, lovingkindness, steadfast love, mercy, kindness, great kindness, commitment, goodness, and favor. More than any other word in the Bible, *hesed* describes God's attitude toward sinful humanity. Its character is such that God will not let us go and leave us to our well-

---

7 A study of the word *hesed* could transform your life. For such a study, see the first Personal Application Project at the end of this booklet.

deserved ruin. Its quality is such that the psalmist considered God's *hesed* (translated here as "steadfast love") to be "better than life" (Psalm 63:3).

It may be that you are reading this booklet as a believer in Jesus Christ. If so, you are undoubtedly rejoicing in God's *hesed*. But if you have never considered Christianity or are unsure of your personal relationship with God, please take the time to consider these matters. Spiritual issues are always of extreme importance, no matter a person's life circumstance. But for anyone suffering with a terminal illness it is all the more critical to have time and space to reflect on everything that is of importance in life. Some of the practical points mentioned earlier in the booklet may encourage such opportunities by helping you to maximize your time and energy.

In the midst of ever-changing circumstances remember that nothing can deter or defeat God's *hesed*. Even our unfaithfulness to God is met with God's faithfulness to himself in creating us, redeeming us, and preserving us for himself. It was in that divinely inspired confidence that the apostle Paul wrote,

> I am sure that neither death nor life, nor
> angels nor rulers, nor things present nor

things to come, nor powers, nor height nor
depth, nor anything else in all creation, will
be able to separate us from the love of God
in Christ Jesus our Lord.

(Romans 8:38–39)

And it is God's *hesed* that creates a foundation of
hope for every person who repents of sin and places
his or her faith in the Lord Jesus as Savior.

The Foundation of Hope

Many Bible authors wrote to alleviate the anguish endured by fellow believers. For example, in what is commonly known as the "Hall of Faith," the writer of Hebrews uses well-known heroes in chapter 11 to demonstrate God's faithfulness in difficult circumstances. He sums up his catalog with the words,

> Therefore, since we are surrounded by so great a cloud of witnesses ... let us run with endurance the race that is set before us.
>
> (Hebrews 12:1)

On the surface it would seem as though the author is encouraging us to look to past or present runners. He is not. He is directing our attention to God himself. He is the sustainer of all who "run

The Foundation of Hope

with endurance the race that is set before us." Our attention should not be focused on other mortals, but on the incarnate God, "Jesus, the founder and perfecter of our faith, who ... endured the cross, despising the shame, and is seated at the right hand of the throne of God" (v. 2). The witnesses are not witnesses of our race and we are not witnesses of their race. We are all witnesses of the enduring grace of God. Trials prove the sufficiency of God's grace in any difficulty. The center of our attention is the God who was faithful to earlier believers and will likewise be faithful to us.

Abel's bust is the first one we see as we enter the Hall of Faith, but at the end of the chapter the writer provides a generic record of unnamed people who

> ... conquered kingdoms, enforced justice, obtained promises, stopped the mouths of lions, quenched the power of fire, escaped the edge of the sword, were made strong out of weakness, became mighty in war, put foreign armies to flight ... received back their dead by resurrection ...
>
> (11:33–35)

At this point, right in the middle of verse 35, the

author's tone changes. The remainder of these heroes appear as victims, not victors. He writes,

> Some were tortured, refusing to accept
> release, so that they might rise again to
> a better life. Others suffered mocking
> and flogging, and even chains and
> imprisonment. They were stoned, they
> were sawn in two, they were killed with the
> sword. They went about in skins of sheep
> and goats, destitute, afflicted, mistreated—
> of whom the world was not worthy—
> wandering about in deserts and mountains,
> and in dens and caves of the earth.
>
> (vv. 35–38)

Every person from verse 1 through verse 35a could be humanly deemed a success. Each hero won, conquered, obtained, and so on. But verse 35b changes everything with the phrase "Some were tortured." Every person thereafter is not successful from a human perspective. The people listed in the second half of the Hall of Faith did not act upon anything, but were acted upon. They did not "win"; in fact, from a human perspective, they lost. They were tortured, imprisoned, and stoned. And yet the

Bible states that the world was not worthy of such people. Even though, from a human viewpoint, they were victims and subject to powers beyond their control, they served as witnesses to the foundation of our hope: God's all-sufficient grace. God is faithful in spite of circumstances. He is our hope, whether we are well or ill, in life or in death.

Jesus Is Our Greatest Hope

It is more than likely that you (or the suffering person you know and love) would not count yourself as belonging among the first half of the heroes of faith. Rather than you acting, much of life may be acting upon you. You probably don't see yourself as a victor over life's circumstances. The terminal illness that afflicts your body may torture you. It may mock any prospect for the future that was once so hopefully planned. Your illness may chain you to a hospital, a house, a chair, or a bed. Yet the writer of Hebrews wants you to know that God's grace is sufficient in spite of your circumstances. Nineteenth-century Scottish pastor Robert Murray McCheyne wrote,

> *Set not your hearts on the flowers of this*
> *world. They shall fade and die. Prize the*

> *Rose of Sharon and the Lily of the Valley*
> *[poetic biblical names for Jesus]. He changes*
> *not! Live nearer to Christ than to any person*
> *on this earth; so that when they are taken,*
> *you may have Him to love and lean upon.*[8]

On the Mount of Transfiguration, as Jesus discussed his own death with Peter, James, and John, he was intentionally flanked by Moses and Elijah (Matthew 17:1–8; Mark 9:2–8). Moses' death is recorded in Scripture, but the Bible teaches that Elijah entered heaven alive in a flaming chariot. Talking with Moses and Elijah implied that Jesus was the Lord of the living and of the dead. The conversation was intended to encourage the disciples, who would soon witness Jesus's death and not long after suffer their own deaths.

Life and death are the same to God. In the divine economy, anyone who never knows Christ is never alive to God, and anyone who places faith in Christ as Lord and Savior never dies. Whether a person closes his or her eyes in what Paul called "sleep" (1 Corinthians 15:51) or steps into heaven with eyes

8 Robert Murray McCheyne, *The Sermons of the Rev. Robert Murray McCheyne, Minister of St Peter's Church, Dundee* (New York: Robert Carter & Brothers, 1854), 314.

wide open makes no difference to the God in whose presence no one dies. If you read the four Gospels you will find not a single person dying in Jesus's presence. Instead, Jesus raised people from the dead. His divine life did not allow death to prevail. It still does not.

What about when Jesus died on the cross? Didn't the two malefactors die in his presence? Look closely at Golgotha (the hill where Jesus was crucified) as depicted by the inspired authors. One wrote,

> Since it was the day of Preparation, and so that the bodies would not remain on the cross on the Sabbath (for that Sabbath was a high day), the Jews asked Pilate that their legs might be broken and that they might be taken away. So the soldiers came and broke the legs of the first, and of the other who had been crucified with him. But when they came to Jesus and saw that he was already dead, they did not break his legs.
>
> (John 19:31–33)

The soldiers broke the legs of the men on either side of Jesus in order to expedite their deaths, but upon approaching Jesus they discovered that he was

35

already dead. He died before either of the men who were crucified with him. But he did not die before he promised a repentant criminal that death could not keep the dying man from life in God's paradise (Luke 23:43).

In the midst of a terminal illness the foundation of our hope is not our own dreams, strength, or expectations for tomorrow. The blessing of life is a privilege gifted to us and not a right that we have earned. Hence, prolonged anger is misconceived ownership. We get angry when life does not go the way we planned, as though we had the right to plan our lives. But our hope cannot be in our own lives if we intend to be hopeful at all.

Our hope is found in God to whom life and death are the same because his *hesed* provides us with an eternal life; not just an extension of life, but a quality of life that cannot be diminished. Jesus said,

> I came that they may have life and have
> it abundantly.
>
> (John 10:10)

"Winning" against all odds one day and "losing" against pain or procedures the next are not God's criteria for faithful Christian living. Good reports and bad reports do not determine our mental or emotional outlook. Nothing can change God's outcome. Our hope is in the eternal, omnipotent God, not in what we would consider to be his blessings or lack thereof. We rest in God, and in God alone. His plans cannot be defeated. His purposes are steadfast. We are secure in him.

God Is Our Well-Placed Hope

Regardless of how or when we die, we are all going to die. Trusting our health, ingenuity, money, science, medicine, treatments, breakthroughs, or physicians will only disappoint us. One day we are wholly unaware of any reason to be concerned; the next day we are stunned by a terminal diagnosis. One day we are completely surrendered to dying; the next day new research gives birth to the possibility of extended tomorrows. One day we are hoping; the next day, hopeless. Life can be a rollercoaster when we are healthy; an elevator drop when we are not.

Only God is our well-placed hope. Every day of our lives, every person in our lives, every joy of our lives, every success in our lives, every defeat in our lives: everything about our lives is Father-filtered. The uncertainties of life are intended to loosen our grip on what cannot bring us ultimate happiness so that we will then focus on the only Person who will never disappoint us and who alone can offer us infinite joy. It takes a lifetime to prove to us that this life is not all there is. It cannot be all there is. We would not want it to be all there is. Yet it still takes a lifetime to learn this important truth.

There is a peace and joy that are beyond the troubles of this world and independent of anything that occurs here. In spite of their life circumstances, each of the saints in Hebrews 11 witnessed to God's *hesed*, his faithful love which is able to sustain and keep those who repent of their sins and trust in him. Above all, Elijah, Moses, the Hall of Faith men and women, and Christ's own death and resurrection teach us that for Christians it is not death to die. We may suffer, but we do so in a hope that not even death can deny.

> *It is not death to die,*
> *To leave this weary road,*
> *And midst the brotherhood on high*
> *To be at home with God.*
>
> *It is not death to close*
> *The eye long dimmed by tears,*

And wake, in glorious repose,
To spend eternal years.

It is not death to bear
The wrench that sets us free
From dungeon chain, to breathe the air
Of boundless liberty.

It is not death to fling
Aside this sinful dust
And rise, on strong exulting wing,
To live among the just.

Jesus, thou Prince of Life,
Thy chosen cannot die:
Like thee, they conquer in the strife
To reign with thee on high.[9]

9 H. A. César Malan, 1832, *'Non, ce n'est pas mourir que
   d'aller vers son Dieu'*; translated into English by George W.
   Bethune.

Suffering in Hope

As Jenny lay dying she was surrounded by family and friends. Her church small group cared for her by providing meals and around-the-clock ministry. Stan and Jenny's family forsook their own homes and jobs to pay their respects to a mother, daughter, sister, cousin, aunt, and friend. One family recorded their children reciting Scripture and singing Christian songs, and Stan played the recording for Jenny. We all prayed together multiple times. Family and friends wandered throughout the house, rejoicing in Jenny's life, sharing memories, and encouraging one another through Scripture. She was constantly surrounded by those she loved.

At Stan's request, my wife, Teana, and I sat with him and his two sons, discussing the end-of-life process. Stan asked pertinent questions about Jenny's well-being and his Christian response to her passing.

Everyone present recognized that Jenny's death was only a new and glorious beginning for her. When she died we all cried in sorrow for our loss, yet rejoiced at her gain.

Jenny's funeral began late because of the vast number of people who stood in line to express their love for Stan and his sons. In great wisdom she had preplanned every aspect of her funeral. It was a great kindness from Jenny to Stan and the children that she did so. Every aspect of the service honored God and magnified his grace. Every detail reminded the Christians present of God's all-sufficient grace and pointed unbelievers to Jesus as the source of present hope and lasting joy.

Being Encouraged and Encouraging Others

Rosalind Goforth (1864–1942) served with her missionary husband, Jonathan, in China for many years.[10] As a young pastor I was deeply impressed

---

10 Jonathan Goforth (1859–1936) and Rosalind were the first Canadian Presbyterian missionaries to China. They endured the loss of five of their eleven children during their ministry to that country. The Goforths ministered in China until 1935, only a year before Jonathan's death.

41

with the Goforths' missionary passion and became an acquaintance of their last living child, Mary. For many years I read books about the Goforths to my children during evening devotionals. Rosalind, who knew the danger of entering unexplored China without the comfort of any experienced counsel, once penned the following words:

> *If you have gone a little way ahead of me,*
> > *call back;*
> *'Twill cheer my heart and help my feet along*
> > *the stony track;*
> *And if, perchance, Faith's light is dim,*
> > *because the oil is low,*
> *Your call will guide my lagging course as*
> > *wearily I go.*
>
> *Call back, and tell me that He went with you*
> > *into the storm;*
> *Call back, and say He kept you when the*
> > *forest's roots were torn;*
> *That when the heavens thundered and the*
> > *earthquake shook the hill,*
> *He bore you up and held you where the very*
> > *air was still.*

O friend, call back and tell me, for I cannot
   see your face;
They say it glows with triumph, and your
   feet bound in the race;
But there are mists between us, and my
   spirit eyes are dim,
And I cannot see the glory, though I long for
   word of Him.

But if you'll say He heard you when your
   prayer was but a cry,
And if you'll say He saw you through the
   night's sin-darkened sky;
If you have gone a little way ahead, O friend,
   call back;
'Twill cheer my heart and help my feet along
   the stony track.[11]

Others may call back to you. I trust that you will also call back to others. Share your faith, your doubts, and your fears. Talk about the joys and sorrows of life. Counsel offered at the end of life has a unique perspective that should not be hoarded or wasted.

---

11 Rosalind Goforth, "Call Back!," in *Climbing: Memories of a Missionary's Wife*; available at http://www.baptistbible believers.com/Books/ClimbingMemoriesofAMissionaries Wife1945/tabid/218/Default.aspx.

When one of our extended family members was diagnosed with cancer, my wife, Teana, spoke with her about optional medications that, if taken simultaneous to her chemotherapy, would reduce sickness and vomiting. The family member was unaware of such options, but on Teana's advice asked her physician for this medication. The physician gladly complied and our loved one experienced amazing results. Paul intimated this kind of care when he wrote,

> Blessed be the God and Father of our
> Lord Jesus Christ, the Father of mercies
> and God of all comfort, who comforts
> us in all our affliction, so that we may
> be able to comfort those who are in any
> affliction, with the comfort with which we
> ourselves are comforted by God. For as we
> share abundantly in Christ's sufferings,
> so through Christ we share abundantly in
> comfort too.

> (2 Corinthians 1:3–5)

Several months before writing this booklet I shared my thoughts on terminal illness with several confidants. A physician friend then approached me and asked for an extended conversation. His tear-filled eyes demonstrated how difficult it is for a doctor to "change the conversation" from ongoing care to palliative care: to actually begin talking about end-of-life concerns with people who do not want to believe, think about, or discuss such things. He spoke with great passion about the ongoing trauma faced by doctors who daily and caringly inform patients and families that life expectancy is severely diminished and that, in the best interests of the patient, the family should recognize the reality of their loved one's impending death and make medical and other appropriate preparations.

Christ's Triumphant Ministry through Us

I understand that particular physician's sincere heartache. But the gospel offers surpassing joy to accompany our deepest sorrows. The gospel is God's good news about abundant and eternal life through repentance and faith in Jesus. Christianity enables us to suffer differently from non-Christians. We are, as Paul says, "more than conquerors through him who loved us" (Romans 8:37). In another text Paul described the way we experience triumph in the midst of apparent defeat as a "triumphal procession" (2 Corinthians 2:14).

Both those phrases served as verbal pictures of an event well known to the people of the apostle's era. Victorious Roman generals returned to the capital city in a triumphal procession much akin to the ticker-tape parade of a championship sports team in New York City. The emperor joined innumerable Romans as they lined the city's streets and gratefully and loudly cheered the conquering hero. Clad in regalia worthy of a king, and carrying the scepter of power and the olive branch of peace, the conqueror rode in a gilded horse-drawn chariot. His vast army followed him, hailing him and shouting, "Behold the triumph!" All the wealth of the conquered nation was placed on public display in the parade. Behind the triumphant army and the seized treasure the conqueror's prisoners were forced to walk through the city streets as living demonstrations of the certain defeat of all Rome's enemies. The triumphant procession wound its way through the city, finally arriving at the Circus Maximus, where the defeated monarch was placed on display for mockery and personally executed by the conquering Roman general. Vanquished soldiers of the defeated army were then led into the public arena to fight wild beasts, all for the amusement of the Roman empire and to generate awe among Rome's potential enemies. In the end, the conquering Roman general stood alone to receive the applause and adulation of Rome's citizenry.

In like manner, Jesus leads his people into the celestial city (heaven) as victors over any enemy foolish enough to confront God's omnipotence— even death. In that city, sin is obsolete, death is powerless, and sorrow is foreign. It is interesting that Paul reminds us that

> Christ *always* leads us in triumphal
> procession, and through us spreads
> the fragrance of the knowledge of
> him everywhere.
>   (2 Corinthians 2:14, emphasis added)

We do not wait until we arrive in heaven for the triumph of our lives to be experienced, known, or shared. The procession itself is triumphant. The Roman general joyfully led his conquering troops toward the Circus Maximus. Our lives and deaths are also triumphant demonstrations of God's grace. The great joy of our lives is that we believe "to die is gain" (Philippians 1:21). Such realities cannot help but change the way we live and die. The end

47

of this life is only the beginning of an eternal life in God's presence for those who trust in Jesus Christ's death and resurrection on their behalf. And the transition occurs faster than an eye can blink (1 Corinthians 15:52).

When my grandfather was rushed to the emergency room in his hometown of Laurel, Mississippi, my dad immediately left San Antonio, Texas, but he did not arrive before my grandfather died. However, Dad's siblings were in the room with Granddaddy and later relayed the following story to my father, whose family nickname was "Buddy." A swinging door opened into Granddaddy's room in the ER. Every time the door swung open my grandfather would look in that direction and ask, "Buddy?" One time when that door swung open, Granddaddy vainly looked in its direction for my father; by the time it swung back the other way, my grandfather was already in heaven.

Absent from the Body, Present with the Lord

On one occasion the apostle Paul wrote,

> We are of good courage, and we would
> rather be away from the body and at home

with the Lord.

(2 Corinthians 5:8)

For Christians, to "be away from the body" is to be "at home with the Lord." There is no time delay and no intermediary place. One moment we are on earth; the next we are in heaven. We are with loved ones, then we are with the Lord. We are in pain, then painless. We are fearful, then full of faith. We are blinded by sorrow, and then we see the Lord. One moment we are wondering about the future; the next moment we are in that future. Contemplating this reality Paul exclaimed,

> *So we do not lose heart. Though our*
> *outer self is wasting away, our inner self*
> *is being renewed day by day. For this light*
> *momentary affliction is preparing for*
> *us an eternal weight of glory beyond all*
> *comparison, as we look not to the things*
> *that are seen but to the things that are*
> *unseen. For the things that are seen are*
> *transient, but the things that are unseen*
> *are eternal.*

(2 Corinthians 4:16–18)

49

With such certainty awaiting us, why would we lose heart?

Illness Is Not Wasted by God

We may not know how we will die or when we will die, but we know that "it is not death to die." Christ's passion and resurrection provide us with unfaltering assurances. His suffering speaks volumes to your own illness. God planned Jesus's death. Although it was carried out by evil men, it accomplished good. God is not taken by surprise. Suffering is a part of his grand scheme. No suffering or heartache is wasted. There are purposes beyond our recognition. Life and death are subject to God alone. God is not indifferent to your illness. Death is not the end of life. For the Christian, what is beyond death is worth more than anything endured in this life.

These assurances all spring from Jesus's own suffering, life, death, and resurrection. He provides hope, peace, and joy as we travel as pilgrims toward home. Various versions of Scripture call Christians *pilgrims* to remind us of our temporal existence on earth. A person leaving home might be a runaway. An individual with no home might be a vagabond. But a person going home is a pilgrim. And what a home! Until then, your hope is founded in Christ's resurrection and ascension to God's right hand, where he sovereignly rules everything in a manner characteristic of the reasons we love him. It is a well-founded hope because it is in a person: the one who lived, died, and lives forever.

When Peter wrote to encourage his suffering readers he used a term to describe God that took their attention all the way back to the beginning of everything in existence. He called God the "faithful Creator." He wrote,

> Let those who suffer according to God's
> will entrust their souls to a faithful Creator
> while doing good.
>
> (1 Peter 4:19)

The ramifications of such encouragement are enormous. Only when the sun lacks light, the moon ceases to rise, the tide has no bounds, and mountains crumble should we doubt God's love or care. As long as creation exists it shouts that God is in control, loving, and faithful. This understanding frees us to "do good" while we are suffering. We don't have to control our health, or the manner or day of our death. Hoping in God enables us to carry on with what is important in our lives, enabling us to do good while we are alive: to call back or call over to others. The same grace of faith from God gives us unceasing, overflowing joy. It moves us from self-indulgence or self-pity into self-sacrifice. This causes believers and unbelievers alike to marvel at God's amazing, sustaining, all-sufficient grace. It challenges the faith of some and inspires the faith of others. And it all points to Jesus Christ.

William Cowper, an 18th-century English poet and hymnwriter, experienced this grace and wrote about it. Cowper suffered from severe depression and was often bedbound for months. Yet it was through his depression that he acknowledged the Lord Jesus Christ as his personal Savior. In the midst of such recurring depression, Cowper often saw the light of God's grace. On one occasion he wrote,

> *God moves in a mysterious way*
> *His wonders to perform;*
> *He plants His footsteps in the sea,*
> *And rides upon the storm.*
>
> *Deep in unfathomable mines*
> *Of never-failing skill*
> *He treasures up His bright designs*
> *And works His sovereign will.*

Ye fearful saints, fresh courage take;
The clouds ye so much dread
Are big with mercy, and shall break
In blessings on your head.

Judge not the Lord by feeble sense,
But trust Him for His grace;
Behind a frowning providence
He hides a smiling face.

His purposes will ripen fast,
Unfolding every hour;
The bud may have a bitter taste,
But sweet will be the flower.

Blind unbelief is sure to err,
And scan His work in vain;
God is His own interpreter,
And He will make it plain.[12]

12 William Cowper, *Olney Hymns*, 1779.

CONCLUSION

On May 19, 1780, a day now known as New England's Dark Day, the Connecticut House of Representatives (USA) sat in session with the full benefit of the natural light expressed in a bright and sunny spring day. Unbeknown to the men at work, God's sovereign hand would soon overshadow their work through an eclipse of the sun. Taken by surprise, many in the chamber surmised that the Second Coming of Jesus had begun. The panic of the moment created differing responses from that austere group of men. Many wanted to pray, some wanted to adjourn proceedings so as to be with family or conduct final personal business, while others were paralyzed with fear or remorse.

In the midst of that chaos, the Speaker of the House arose to say,

... "This well may be
The Day of Judgment which the
*   world awaits;*
But be it so or not, I only know
My present duty, and my Lord's command
To occupy till He come. So at the post
Where He hast set me in His providence,
I choose, for one, to meet Him face to face,
No faithless servant frightened from
*   my task,*
But ready when the Lord of the harvest calls;
And therefore, with all reverence, I
*   would say,*
Let God do His work, we will see to ours.
Bring in the candles."[13]

The gospel is God's candle. It provides light in the midst of any darkness. It supplies answers to our most important questions. It may very well be that the illness facing you has darkened your horizon. God's face may often be difficult to perceive. But in this momentary darkness it is my prayer that you will be found as "no faithless servant frightened"

13 Quoted by John Greenleaf Whittier in his poem "Abraham Davenport," in *The Tent on the Beach, and Other Poems* (Boston: Ticknor & Fields, 1867).

from your calling to faith, hope, and joy. Remember the gospel and its sufficiency. Today you may rejoice in God. That joy may adequately reflect God's grace. Tomorrow you may be overwhelmed by sadness. Your sadness may cause you to doubt God's existence or sufficiency. Yet good days or bad days do not threaten the reality of the gospel. The gospel is not without power. Do not think the success of the gospel for your family or friends rests in your strength. God will reveal the gospel in both your strength and your weakness. He is the only Savior. It may very well be your weakest point or worst day that best showcases why we all need a Savior.

Some days we smile and sing; other days we grunt and bear with our decaying bodies. Some days we slay lions; other days the lions feast. Nevertheless, God is faithful, and truth is unalterable and eternal. The Bible is the revelation of a God who does not fail, but who nonetheless reveals himself through fallen people. Our trust is not in our knowledge, ability, or strength, but in God's wisdom and power. Remember, your hope in all things is drawn from that eternal spring of everything God is and will be for you in Jesus Christ, his Son and your Savior.

Personal Application Projects

1. The following biblical references for the word
    hesed are taken from a comprehensive list in an
    article by Norman H. Snaith, in *A Theological
    Word Book of the Bible*.[14] Reading these texts
    will encourage your heart in the experience of
    God's boundless kindness.

    Genesis 39:21; Exodus 34:6–7; Psalms 23:6;
    40:10–11; 89:1–2; 118:1–4; 145:8; Jeremiah 31:3;
    Jonah 4:2.

2. What has your study of God's *hesed* revealed?
    How has it changed the way you view God? How
    does it change your view of your illness?

3. If you are wondering why God has seen fit for
    you to suffer in this way or wonder if you can
    continue, read 2 Corinthians 12:8–10. Was Paul's
    suffering recurrent? How did God explain his
    purposes? What was Paul's reaction to God's

14 Edited by Alan Richardson (New York: Macmillan, 1951),
   136–137.

plan? Why did he rejoice in his weaknesses?

4. Romans 8:18–26 explains God's purposes in suffering. How many can you find? Why does Paul think that temporal suffering is worth enduring? How does that encourage your heart? What does Paul say that the hope of redemption will do for you? Who helps you in your weaknesses? Take time now to pray for God's Spirit to make these truths real in your life.

5. In John 17:1–4 Jesus stated that his "hour" had arrived. What did he mean? How does knowing that God ordains suffering for his glory and your good affect you? How will you apply that truth to your life? Take time now to look around and consider whom you are influencing and how.

6. The cross is a symbol of justice and love. It also reveals the kind of God we trust. How does the thought of Jesus willingly suffering for those he loves encourage you in your suffering? What does it say about the purposes of suffering? How does knowing that Jesus suffered and trusted God increase your faith?

7. Hebrews 4:14–16 and 5:7–9 describe Jesus's suffering and the benefits we derive from his

sacrifice. What were the consequences for Jesus and others that God sent him to Calvary? How does Jesus's suffering help you relate to him? How is Jesus able to relate to us because he has suffered? What may you receive as a result of his suffering?

8. People often think that suffering is unfair. How does Ezekiel 18:25–29 answer that charge? What does Jesus's death say about fairness? Was the cross fair? If God was "fair," what would we all deserve and how would God treat us? How does this change your view of suffering and grace?

9. Read Hebrews 11:1–12:2. What do the witnesses in the Hall of Faith witness to? How can you witness to God's grace? Consider journaling the various ways in which God has met you with his grace. Such a journal would be a wonderful gift for a family member one day.

10. Consider rereading this booklet, paying particular attention to the biblical references. Take time to journal your thoughts about them. What does God say in each passage? What is the meaning of each passage? How does each passage relate to you?

Where Can I Get Further Help?

Many people have written for the encouragement of those suffering with terminal illness and their families. Any of the following resources are helpful if you are suffering with a terminal illness, or if you have a family member or loved one with such an illness.

Alcorn, Randy, *If God Is Good: Faith in the Midst of Suffering and Evil* (Colorado Springs, CO: Multnomah, 2009). Alcorn writes that evil comes from human rebellion or sin, and suffering is a secondary evil brought on by that primary evil. Nevertheless, God intends an eternal good through both evil and suffering.

Carson, D. A., *How Long, O Lord? Reflections on Suffering and Evil* (2nd edn.; Grand Rapids: Baker Academic, 2006). Offers a biblical analysis of suffering and is unique because it does not attempt to provide answers the Bible does not give.

Edwards, Brian H., *Horizons of Hope: Reality in Disability* (rev. edn.; Leominster: Day One, 2005). Confronts long-term disability with God's comfort and sovereignty. It is highlighted by the author's own testimony as well as the testimonies of others who have dealt with this issue.

Lewis, C. S., *The Problem of Pain* (New York: HarperOne, 2001). Answers the timeless and universal question, "Why would an all-loving, all-powerful, all-knowing God allow people to experience pain?" It is not light reading but is written by someone who experienced his subject matter firsthand. Lewis writes out of that pain for fellow sufferers.

MacArthur, John, *The Power of Suffering: Strengthening Your Faith in the Refiner's Fire* (Colorado Springs: David C. Cook, 2011). Challenges assumptions about suffering and helps people better understand the unique and important role suffering plays in life. It also prepares readers to comfort and encourage others.

Sproul, R. C., *Surprised by Suffering: The Role of Pain and Death in the Christian Life* (rev. edn.; Orlando: Reformation Trust, 2009). Part 1 explains God's presence in suffering. Part 2 summarizes what happens after death.

Tautges, Paul, *Comfort Those Who Grieve: Ministering God's Grace in Times of Loss* (Leominster: Day One, 2009). Offers pastors and other compassionate caregivers a very biblical and immensely practical resource in how to comfort hurting and dying people.

Walker, Austin, *God's Care for the Widow: Encouragement and Wisdom for Those Who Grieve* (Leominster: Day One, 2010). Provides counsel and comfort for those who live after the death of a husband.

The National Hospice and Palliative Care Organization (NHPCO) promotes a campaign called "It's About How You Live." It encourages people to 1) learn about options for end-of-life care; 2) implement plans to ensure their wishes are honored; 3) voice decisions to family, friends, and health-care providers; and 4) engage others in conversations about the importance of advance-care planning. Visit their Web site, www.nhpco.org, for many other helpful insights.

Booklets in the *Help!* series include ...

(More titles in preparation)